DISCOVER THROUGH CRAFT

SPACE

By Louise Spilsbury

W
FRANKLIN WATTS
LONDON•SYDNEY

First published in 2014 by Franklin Watts
Franklin Watts
338 Euston Road
London NW1 3BH

Franklin Watts Australia
Level 17/207 Kent Street
Sydney, NSW 2000

Series editor: Amy Stephenson
Series designer: Jeni Child
Crafts: Rita Storey
Craft photography: Tudor Photography
Picture researcher: Diana Morris

Picture Credits:
a40757/istockphoto: 19t. Actionphotos/Shutterstock: 12b. angelinast/istockphoto: 7b. Giovanni Benintende/Shutterstock: front cover c b/g. bluecrayola/Shutterstock: 16b. Blue Ring Media/ Shutterstock: 20c. Bobboz/istockphoto: 10. G Breezy/Shutterstock: front cover tr. Marcel Clemens/Shutterstock: 15tcr. courtyandpix/ istockphoto: 23t. John David/Alamy: 4. Sebastien Decoret/Photos. com: 24c. s decoret/Shutterstock: 19b. eta: 11tr. Hubble: 15bl, 15bcl, 15bcr, 26b. istackphotons/istockphoto: 11bl. JohnofParis/ Shutterstock: 26t. NASA: 15tl, 15tcl, 15tr, 15cl, 15cr, 15br, 16t, 16c, 18, 22, 23c, 24t, 27tl, 27tr, 28br, 31, 32. NASA, ESA: 5b, 6, 7t. NASA, ESA, and The Hubble Heritage Team: 5t, 30. NASA, ESA, and The Hubble Heritage Team (AURA/STScl): 1. NASA/JPL/ Caltech: 28t. Nuttapong/Dreamstime: 11tr. Orla/Shutterstock: 14. Rastan/istockphoto: 12t. Vadim Sadovski/Shutterstock:8b. stereo spacecraft: 8t. Shutterhappy images 2007: 23b. Johan Swanepol/ istockphoto: 11tl. Triff/Shutterstock: 20b.

Dewey number: 523.2

HB ISBN: 978 1 4451 3100 9
Library ebook ISBN: 978 1 4451 3587 8

Printed in China

Franklin Watts is a division of Hachette
Children's Books, an Hachette UK company.
www.hachette.co.uk

CONTENTS

Words in **bold** can be found in the glossary on page 30.

Some of the projects in this book require scissors, paint, pins and glue. We would recommend that children are supervised by a responsible adult when using these things.

WHAT'S IN SPACE?

Space contains stars, planets and everything in between, but how did it form?

Huge **telescopes** inside buildings like this one in Arizona, USA, help people to study all of the objects in space.

What was the Big Bang?

The Big Bang is a **theory** about how the **universe** formed. The idea is that about 14 billion years ago, the universe exploded outwards from a hot, **dense** bubble that was smaller than a pinhead. As it spread out, it cooled and tiny bits of **matter** formed. Some of these bits of matter gradually joined together to form the stars and planets.

Each of these areas of light is a whole galaxy. They are different shapes and sizes.

What are galaxies?

The universe contains billions of different **galaxies**. Galaxies are gigantic collections of stars, planets, clouds of **gas** and dust and other matter that are grouped together by a **force** called **gravity**. Gravity is a force that pulls two objects towards each other.

The Milky Way

We live in a galaxy called the Milky Way. It contains Earth, the other planets in our solar system (p. 10) and about 200 billion stars, including the Sun (p. 6). It is shaped like a spiral, but from Earth it doesn't look like a spiral because we are inside it. Almost everything that we can see in the sky is part of the vast Milky Way, but without a telescope we cannot see all of its stars because most of them are so far away from us.

If we could see the Milky Way from the outside, it would look a bit like this spiral-shaped galaxy, called NCG 3949.

Quick *FACTS*

- The universe formed after the 'Big Bang'.
- There are billions of galaxies in the universe.
- Our galaxy is called the Milky Way.

THE SUN AND STARS

The Sun is our nearest star. Like all other stars it gives off heat and light.

Clouds of hot gas can be many different colours.

Stars make heat and light

Stars form from clouds of scorching hot gases. The centre of each cloud gets hotter and hotter until it explodes and forms a star. A star is a ball of constantly exploding gases. The gases mix together and explode again and again. These giant explosions release light and heat **energy** into the universe, which is why stars glow.

Big and small, hot and cold

Stars are all **spherical** (ball-shaped) but they are different sizes. The smallest are about 20 to 40 kilometres wide, but the biggest stars are over 1,000,000,000 (one billion) kilometres wide! The colour of a star depends on how hot or cold it is. Cooler stars glow red, while hotter stars glow blue.

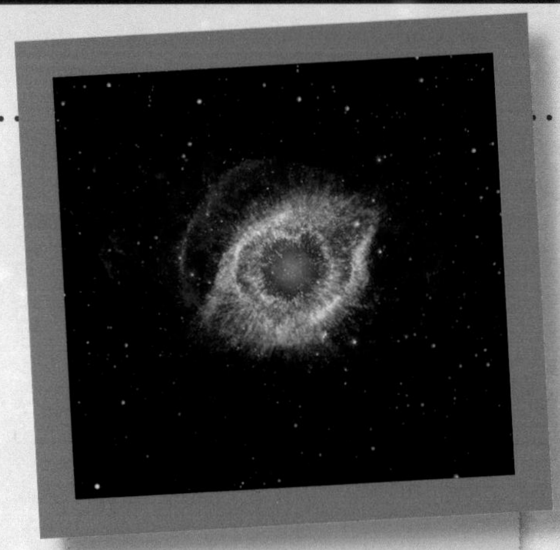

The red star in the centre of this picture is cooling down because it is dying.

The constellation of Orion looks like a man holding a club and a shield.

Star patterns

Some groups of bright stars form patterns in the night sky when you join them up like a dot-to-dot picture. We call these patterns **constellations**. Long ago, people named the constellations after animals, characters from ancient **myths** and other objects. We still use these names today, such as Orion the hunter and Taurus the bull.

HAVE A GO

On a clear night, go outside to see if you can spot any constellations. Ask an adult to take you to a place where there are few streetlights to spoil the view. You can print a map of the stars for where you live to take with you (p. 31).

? What makes the Sun a special star to us? Turn the page to find out.

The Sun is our star

The Sun is almost 1,400,000 kilometres wide. This is huge compared to the size of Earth, which is about 12,700 kilometers wide. But the Sun is really just an ordinary, medium-sized star. It looks bigger and brighter than other stars because it is the nearest star to Earth. The Sun is about 145 million kilometres from Earth, but the next nearest star is 1,000 times further away. It would take more than four light years (see below) to reach this star from Earth. Our Sun also gives us the heat and light we need to survive on Earth.

! It's dangerous to look directly at the Sun because its bright light can damage your eyes.

LIGHT YEARS

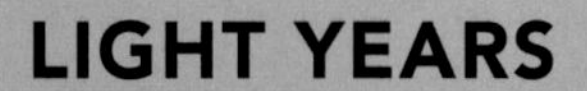

A light year is how far light can travel in one year – almost 10 trillion kilometres!

Quick *FACTS*

- All stars are balls of exploding gas.
- The nearest star to Earth is the Sun.
- Constellations are patterns in the night sky made out of stars.

QUIZ TIME!

How long does it take for light from the Sun to reach Earth?

a. eight minutes

b. eight weeks

c. eight years

Answer on page 32.

Make this

Constellations are a fun way to learn about the stars in the night sky. They are often named after gods, goddesses and characters from myths. Make this constellation of Orion, the hunter, using pins and string.

This picture of Orion is fairly simple. There are actually lots more stars that make up this constellation. What can you find out about the stars that belong to Orion, such as Betelgeuse, or the stars near his belt?

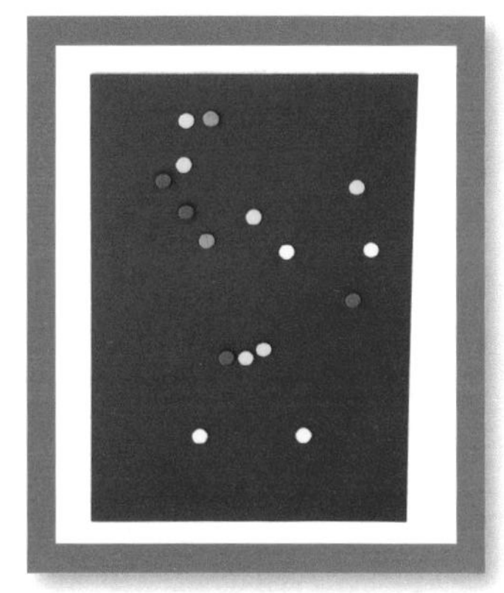

1 Glue a sheet of blue paper to a piece of corrugated card. Copy the pattern of the stars by carefully pushing pins into the paper as shown. Or you can download a star chart (p. 31) to copy a different constellation, such as the Great Bear.

2 Tape a loop of string onto the back of your card.

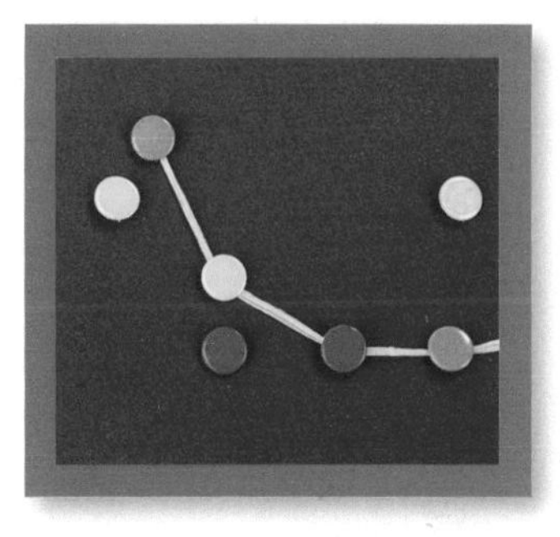

3 Join the pins together with string. Make sure you join the right pins to each other or your constellation won't look right. Remember, some pins may join up to several other pins.

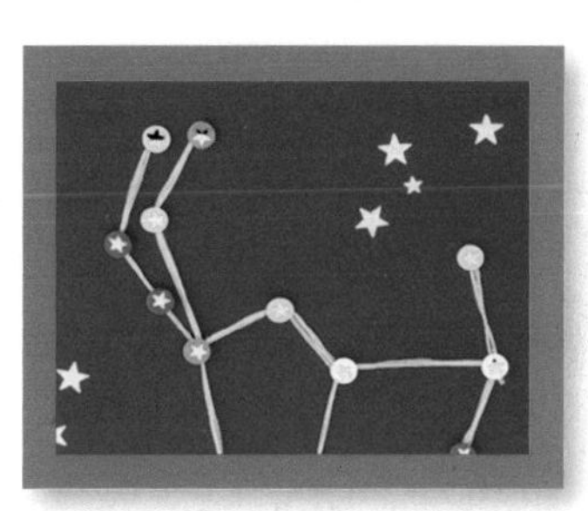

4 Decorate your constellation picture with stick-on stars. Hang up your picture.

THE SOLAR SYSTEM

The solar system is the Sun and all the other objects – such as the planets – that move around it.

Why objects orbit the Sun

Orbiting is when an object, such as a planet (p. 14) goes round and round another object. The Sun, which is in the centre of our solar system, is the biggest and heaviest object in it. The Sun is big, so its pull of gravity is very powerful. The Sun's gravity pulls all of the objects in the solar system, including the planets, towards it so they end up orbiting around it.

HAVE A GO

Spin a ball on a string above your head. The ball is like a planet and you are like the Sun. The ball wants to fly off in a straight line but the string you are holding, like the Sun's gravity, is pulling on it and keeping the ball in orbit around your head!

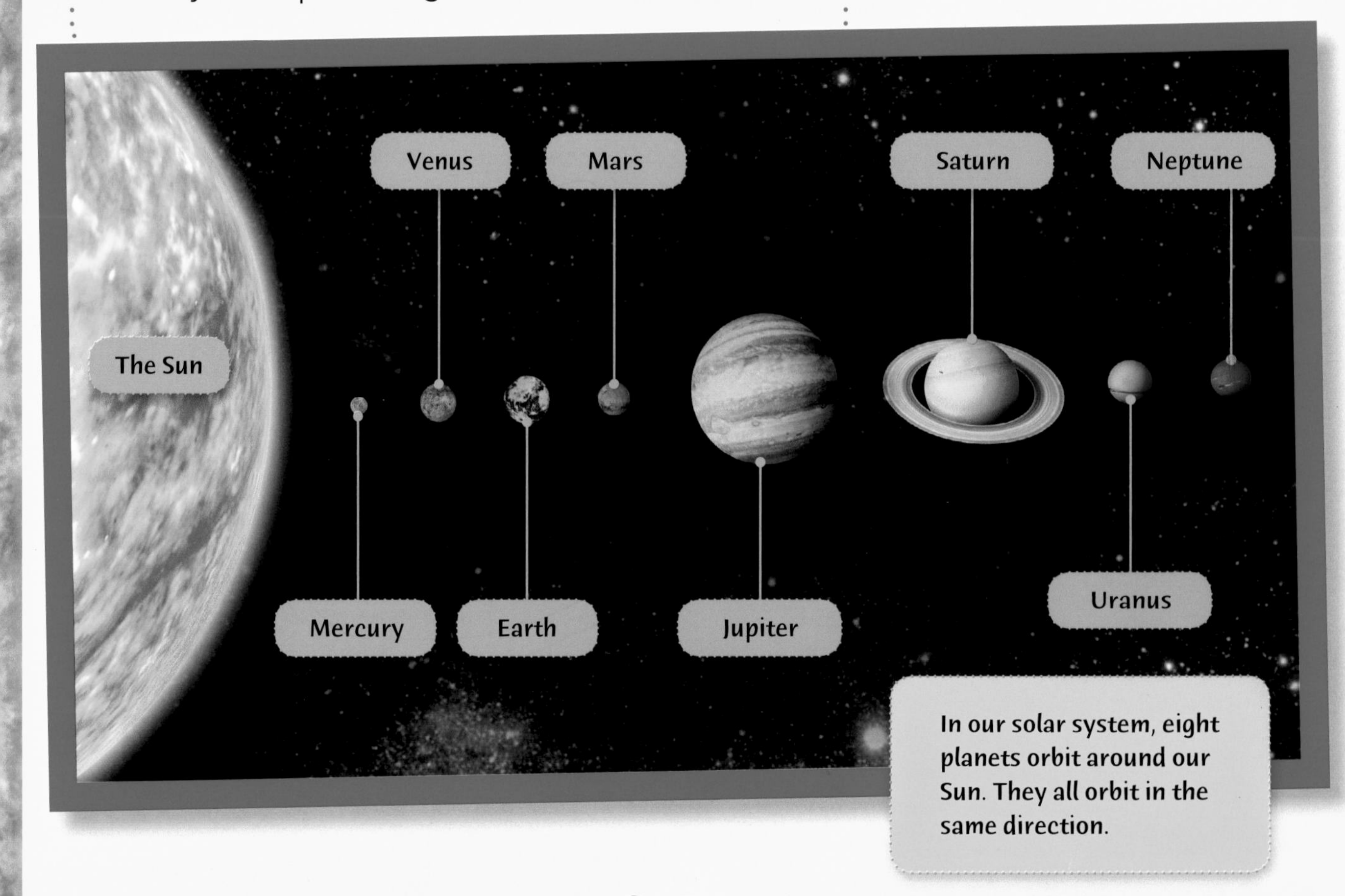

In our solar system, eight planets orbit around our Sun. They all orbit in the same direction.

Asteroids

There are other objects in the solar system, too. Asteroids are large rocks that orbit the Sun but are too small to be called planets. They range in size from 10 kilometres to 600 kilometres across. There are many thousands of asteroids in space and at least one new asteroid is spotted by **astronomers** every year!

Meteors or 'shooting stars' zooming across a night sky.

Asteroids are giant chunks of rock left over from when the planets formed 4.5 billion years ago.

Meteoroids

Meteoroids are bits of space rock that range in size from a grain of dust to the size of a house. Meteoroids orbit the Sun too, but if they stray into a planet's **atmosphere** they burn up. The flash of light we see when this happens is called a meteor. We sometimes call them 'shooting stars' because they are so bright, but they are not stars at all. Meteriods that pass through a planet's atmosphere without burning up and reach its surface are called meteorites. Most of the meteorites that fall on Earth are small.

? What else is out there in the solar system? Turn the page to find out.

A comet shoots across the night sky.

Comets

Comets are giant balls of ice, dust and rock in the solar system. When a comet's orbit takes it far from the Sun, it stays icy and frozen. When its orbit brings it close to the Sun, the ice inside it heats up so much that it turns into gas. This gas, along with dust and bits of rock blown from the comet, trail behind it like an enormous, glowing tail.

Quick *FACTS*

- Everything in the solar system orbits around the Sun because of its strong pull of gravity.
- Some asteroids, comets and meteoroids can be seen from Earth.
- Meteors are sometimes called 'shooting stars'.

QUIZ TIME!

Huge dents in a planet's surface made by meteorites that crash into them are called:

a. graters

b. craters

c. pits

Answer on page 32.

Make this

There are eight planets in our solar system, all orbiting the Sun. Make this colourful model to help you remember the order of the planets, from the one closest to the Sun to the one furthest away.

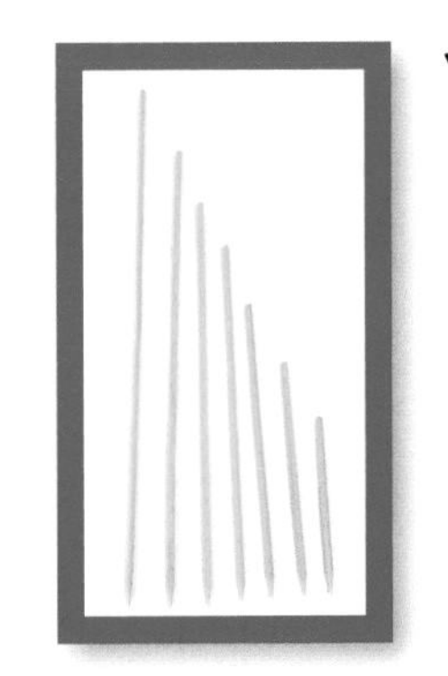

You could add even smaller balls to show the bigger moons that orbit other planets, too.

1 Ask an adult to help you cut eight kebab sticks so that they are all different lengths. (Seven of them are shown here.)

2 Ask an adult to cut a medium-sized polystyrene ball in half. Then cut a circle of paper slightly bigger than the ball. Stick the ball back together with the paper circle sandwiched in between. Paint the planet as shown and leave to dry. (This planet is Saturn.)

3 Paint a big polystyrene ball to look like the Sun. Paint four small balls to look like Mercury, Venus, Earth and Mars. Paint three medium-sized balls to look like Jupiter, Uranus and Neptune. Leave them all to dry.

4 Carefully push a kebab stick into each ball. The shortest one should be in the planet closest to the Sun and the longest one in the planet furthest away from the Sun. Push each of the kebab sticks into the Sun as shown. Put a big piece of plasticine underneath the Sun to keep it in place.

TIP: See p. 10 to make sure the planets are the right colour and in the right order.

THE PLANETS

There are eight planets in our solar system. How are they alike and how are they different?

What is a planet?

A planet is a huge, natural object in space that is spherical and usually orbits a star. The planets in our solar system orbit the Sun. Planets formed from dust and **particles** that slowly joined together over millions of years to make bigger and bigger objects. Planets are usually hotter if they are closer to their star. Planets further from their star are cooler. Venus, a planet in our solar system, is different; it has a thick atmosphere that traps heat like a blanket, making it the hottest planet, even though it is not the closest to the Sun.

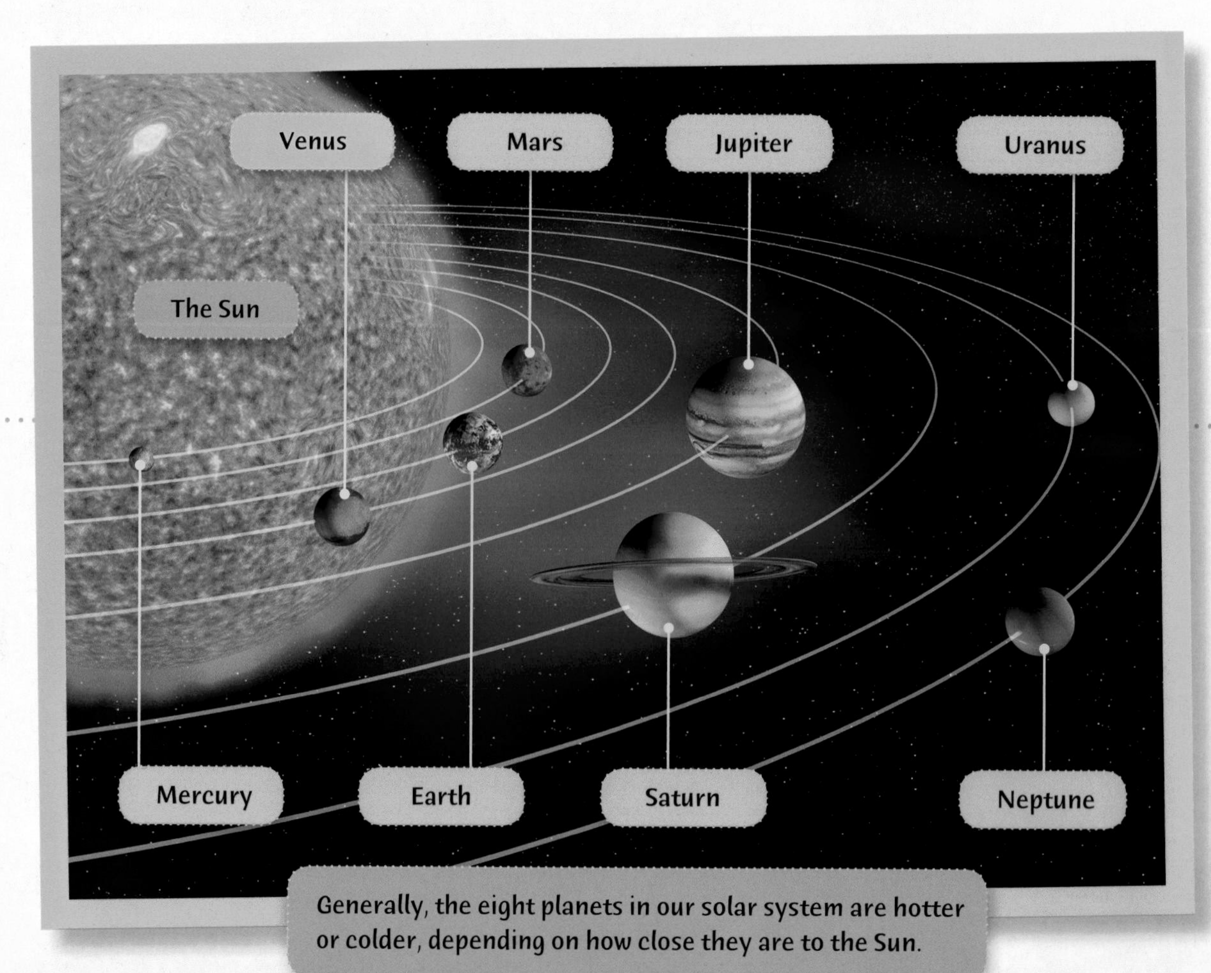

Generally, the eight planets in our solar system are hotter or colder, depending on how close they are to the Sun.

Mercury

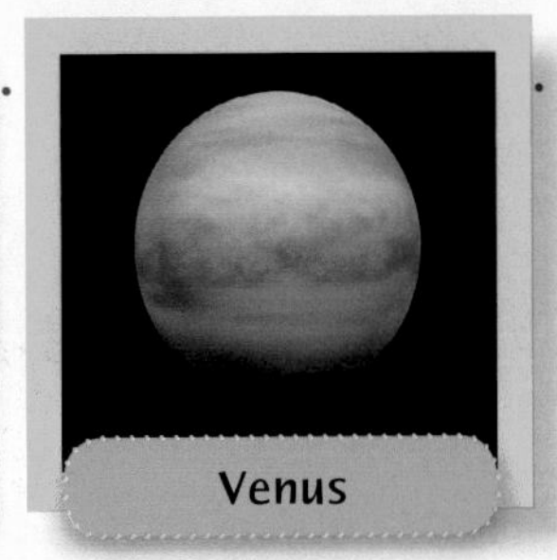

Venus

Earth

Mars

Rocky planets

The four planets closest to the Sun are Mercury, Venus, Earth and Mars. As these planets formed, gases inside them were burned off by heat from the nearby Sun, so they have **solid**, rocky surfaces. These planets have metals in the middle of them. That's why they are small, very heavy for their size and move slowly in their orbits.

Rocky planets, such as Mars, have solid surfaces that a spacecraft could land on.

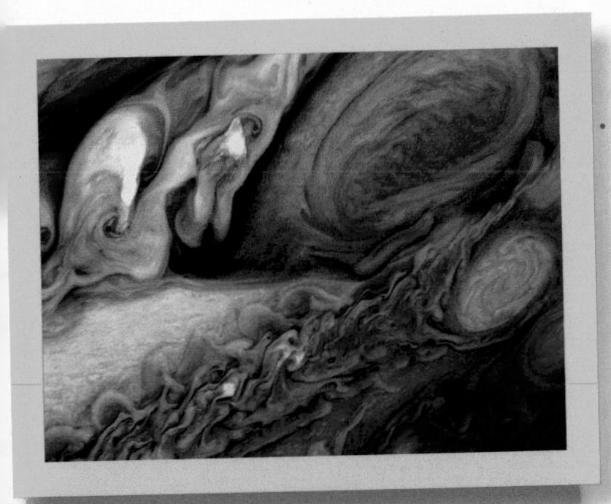

The Great Red Spot is a storm on the planet Jupiter. The storm has been raging for at least 300 years.

Gas giants

The four outer planets – Jupiter, Saturn, Uranus and Neptune – are so far from the Sun that their gases did not burn off as they formed. These planets are giant, spinning balls of gas without a solid surface, although they probably have a rocky **core**. Neptune and Uranus are icy because they are the two furthest planets from the Sun. They all have moons – Jupiter has more than 60!

Jupiter

Saturn

Uranus

Neptune

? Why is Pluto no longer called a planet? Turn the page to find out.

Dwarf planets

Pluto

Pluto was called a planet until 2006. Then astronomers realised there were many similar objects in an area called the Kuiper Belt. They decided a planet is any object with gravity so strong that it can pull smaller, nearby objects towards it, leaving its own orbit clear. Pluto and other objects that haven't got clear orbits are now called dwarf planets.

QUIZ TIME!

What instrument do astronomers use to see the planets and other objects that are far out in space?

- **a. microscope**
- **b. telescope**
- **c. stethoscope**

Answer on page 32.

Cassini Division

Planet rings

Saturn is one of the easiest planets to recognise in our solar system because of the seven main rings that orbit it. The rings are made of lumps of ice, rock and tiny grains of dust. The large gap near the middle of the rings is called the Cassini Division.

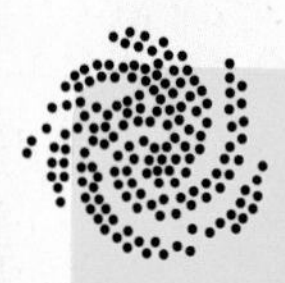

HAVE A GO Planets can be made of solids, **liquids** or gases. Melt an ice cube and then ask an adult to help you boil the water that it melts into. As the water boils, some of the water will **evaporate** and turn into a gas in the air. You have changed a solid into a liquid and a liquid into a gas.

Make this

The rings that orbit around Saturn are some of the most beautiful objects in our solar system. You can make a model of Saturn from a polystyrene ball and an old CD.

Saturn isn't the only planet in our solar system that has rings. Jupiter, Neptune and Uranus also have rings. You could make models of these planets, too.

1 Ask an adult to cut a polystyrene ball in half. Carefully push a cocktail stick into one half. (Note: the ball should be no more than 4 cm in diameter.)

! Make sure you check the CD is not needed before you start!

2

Spread glue around the centre hole on both sides of the CD. Sandwich the CD in between the two halves of the ball. The cocktail stick will help to secure it in place. Spread a ring of glue around the edge of the CD and cover with glitter. Leave to dry.

3

Repeat with a ring of purple glitter. Repeat with more rings of glitter until your CD is covered in rings. Leave to dry then repeat on the other side.

4

Cover both halves of the polystyrene ball with glue and glitter. Leave to dry. Then carefully push a flat, metal drawing pin near the top of the model as shown. Tie some thread around the pin and hang up your model.

EARTH

Earth is special. It's the only planet known to have life on it in our solar system – and in the whole universe!

From space Earth looks like a big, blue ball. That's because 70 per cent of its surface is covered with water.

Life on Earth

One reason there is life on Earth is because it is the only planet in our solar system that has lots of liquid water on its surface. Living things need water. Earth is also the only planet that has an atmosphere with enough **oxygen**, which plants and animals also need to survive. Living things also need sunlight and our planet is exactly the right distance from the Sun, so we get just the right amount.

Keeping warm

Greenhouse gases help to keep our planet warm, in the same way that a greenhouse keeps plants inside it warm.

When heat from the Sun hits the Earth's surface, much of it bounces back into space. But gases in the atmosphere, known as **greenhouse gases**, reflect some of the Sun's heat back to Earth. This keeps Earth at the right temperature for water to stay liquid and for us to live. If Earth were closer to or further away from the Sun, it would either be too hot or too cold to live on our planet!

Day and night

As Earth orbits around the Sun it also rotates, spinning all the way around every 24 hours. The side of Earth that is facing the Sun has daytime and the side of Earth that is turned away from the Sun has night-time. Light can't shine through solid objects, such as the Earth, so the half of Earth that faces the Sun blocks light from getting to the other half.

When one half of Earth has day, the other half has night.

HAVE A GO

Shine a torch on a tennis ball. Part of your ball will be in the light and the other part will be in the shade. What happens if you slowly turn the ball? Did the part that was in the light stay lit or move into the shade? Why do you think this happens?

? How is Earth's orbit around the Sun linked to the seasons? Turn the page to find out.

Seasons

It takes Earth one year to travel all the way around the Sun. The seasons (below) are caused by this orbit around the Sun and because the Earth is tilted at an angle. For some of the year, one half of the Earth is tilted nearer to the Sun so it has warmer weather, called summer. At the same time the other half of the Earth is tilted away from the Sun so it has colder weather, called winter. Seasons also happen in different months around the world, depending on which **hemisphere** you live in. For example, March–May are the spring months in the Northern Hemisphere and the autumn months in the Southern Hemisphere.

Summer
(Winter, Southern Hemisphere)

Spring
(Autumn, Southern Hemisphere)

Sun

Autumn
(Spring, Southern Hemisphere)

Winter
(Summer, Southern Hemisphere)

QUIZ TIME!

Burning fuels, such as oil, releases more greenhouse gases into the atmosphere and makes Earth warmer. What is this effect called?

a. global warming
b. global heating
c. global warning

Answer on page 32.

Quick *FACTS*

- The Earth is the only planet we know of that has life on it.
- It is the perfect distance from the Sun to be neither too hot nor too cold.
- Seasons are caused by Earth orbiting the Sun.

Make this

Sundials are a way to tell the time from the position of the Sun. You could make a sundial for your school or garden. But remember, most sundials aren't that accurate; they can only tell you roughly what time it is.

What else can shadows cast by the Sun tell you? What time of day will it be if the shadows are long? What does a short shadow tell you about the height of the Sun in the sky?

1 Cut two circles of gold card, about the size of a plate. Cut one of the circles in half, then into quarters. Cut each quarter in half so you have eight pieces, all the same size and shape.

2 Stick each of the eight pieces onto the back of the other gold circle. They should form a pattern like the one shown.

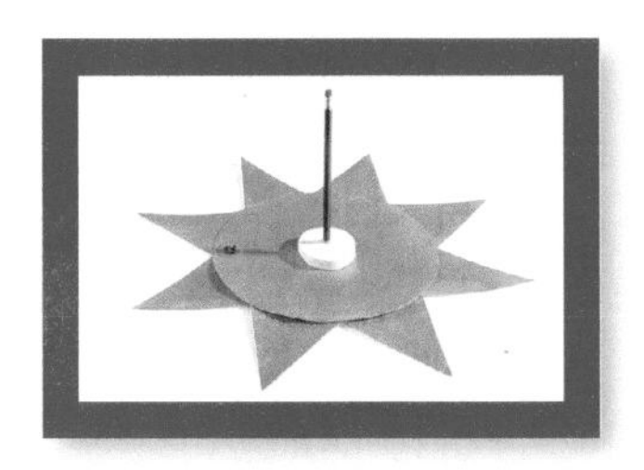

3 Press some plasticine onto the middle of the circle and push a pencil into it. On a sunny day at exactly 12 o'clock put the sundial in the sunshine.

Write the number 12 on a sticker and put the sticker exactly where the shadow of the pencil falls. Make sure you don't move the sundial at all.

4 Leave your sundial outside. Every hour add another sticker where the shadow falls to mark the time. At the end of the day you may have to guess where the rest of the stickers should go.

Or, if you can, you could come back in the morning to finish the rest of them. (Note: you may find that your numbers are not spaced evenly around the dial – this is completely normal!)

THE MOON

The Earth's Moon has orbited our planet for 4.5 billion years. Where did it come from?

How the Moon formed

Astronomers think that our Moon formed when a gigantic object crashed into the new Earth. The impact broke off lots of dust and rubble, which were thrown into space. Attracted by Earth's gravity, these materials began to orbit Earth and eventually joined together to form the Moon. This explains why the Moon's rocks are similar to Earth's.

Earth is much bigger than the Moon. If you imagine the Earth were the size of a tennis ball, the Moon would be the size of a marble!

What is the Moon like?

The Moon is a rocky, spherical object with a solid surface. It has a thin, weak atmosphere, which makes the Moon a cold place with no air or water. There is no weather on the Moon so there are no seasons and no wind or rain. Earth's thick atmosphere burns up meteoroids that enter it, but the Moon's thin atmosphere does not, so it is often hit by meteorites.

The deep craters on the Moon's surface were made by meteorites crashing into it.

Phases of the Moon

The Moon has no light of its own. It shines because it reflects sunlight. The Moon orbits Earth about once every month. It also takes roughly the same amount of time to spin around once on its **axis**. Because of this we always see the same side of the Moon, but we see either more or less of it depending on how much of the sunlit side we can see. The Moon looks like it is changing shape, but it isn't really. We call these shapes the **phases** of the Moon.

The different phases of the Moon that we see each time it orbits Earth.

Quick *FACTS*

• The Moon was formed 4.5 billion years ago. • It has no atmosphere or weather. • The Moon orbits Earth.

? How can the Moon block out the Sun? **Turn the page to find out.**

! A total eclipse is rare and exciting. But NEVER look directly at any type of eclipse. The light from the Sun can damage your eyes.

What is a solar eclipse?

An eclipse is a shadow caused because sunlight cannot pass through dense objects, such as the Moon. The Moon is smaller than the Sun, but because the Sun is so far away, the Moon can still block its light. If the Moon passes between the Sun and the Earth and blocks some of the Sun's light, a shadow of the Moon is cast on the Earth. When only part of the Sun's light is blocked we call this a partial eclipse. There are usually up to five of these every year. A total eclipse – where all of the Sun's light is blocked by the Moon – only happens once every few years.

HAVE A GO

Close one eye and hold a coin at arm's length in front of the other eye. Look at a big object in the distance. Bring the coin slowly towards your eye. Can you still see the big object?

QUIZ TIME!

The Moon and Sun look the same size from Earth. The Moon is 400 times smaller than the Sun, so how far away is the Sun from Earth?

a. 4 times further away
b. 40 times further away
c. 400 times further away?

Answer on page 32.

Make this

You can make a picture using some simple shapes to show the phases of the Moon that we see from Earth.

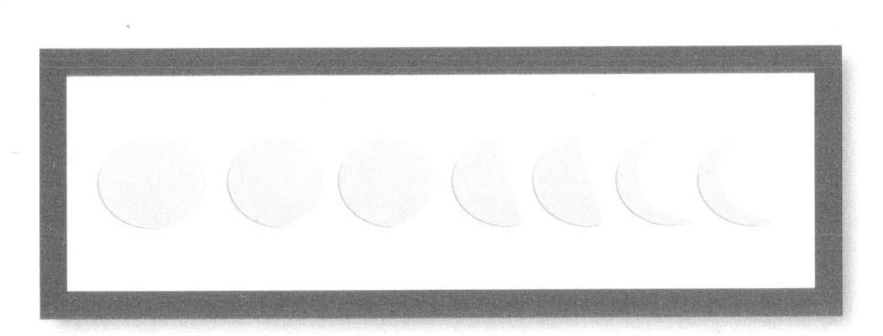

1 Cut out eight black paper circles, all the same size. Cut out four circles from white, shiny paper. They should be the same size as the black circles.

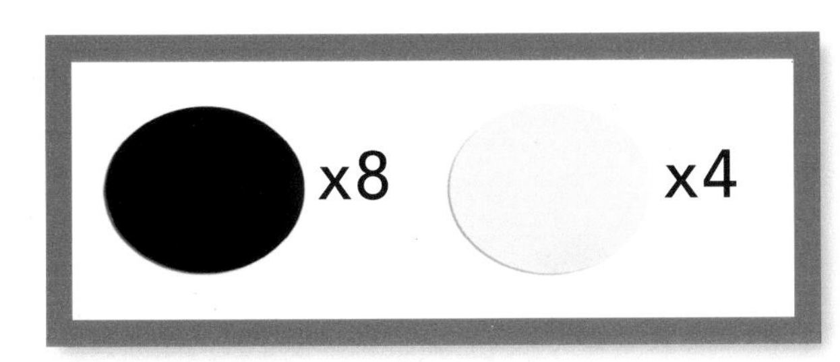

2 Cut one of the shiny white circles in half. Cut a crescent shape (far left) from two of the other shiny circles. You should now have seven shiny white pieces.

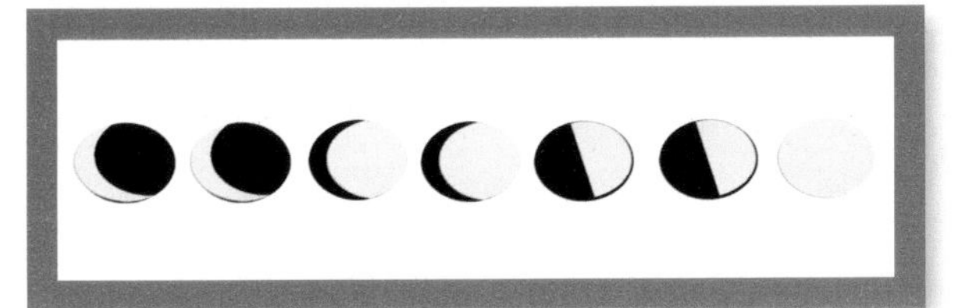

3 Paste all of your white circle sections onto seven of the black circles as shown. Line the edges up neatly. These, along with the full black circle, will be the phases of the Moon.

4 Cut a large semi-circle from blue paper. This will be the Earth. Stick the Earth onto the edge of a piece of black paper. Arrange the Moon shapes around it, in the order shown, to show how much of the Moon you can see during each phase. Put a glitter ring around the full black circle. Decorate your picture with glittery stars.

The black circle with the glittery ring represents the phase of the Moon when we can't see any of the Moon's surface.

EXPLORING SPACE

We know a lot about space because people study and explore it.

Giant telescopes are able to see deep into space.

Telescopes

One way we explore space is with telescopes. Telescopes make faraway objects look closer so we can study them. Astronomers use giant telescopes on Earth and telescopes in space that orbit Earth, such as the Hubble Space Telescope. Space telescopes show us more, partly because the clouds and atmosphere above Earth make it harder for astronomers to see into space.

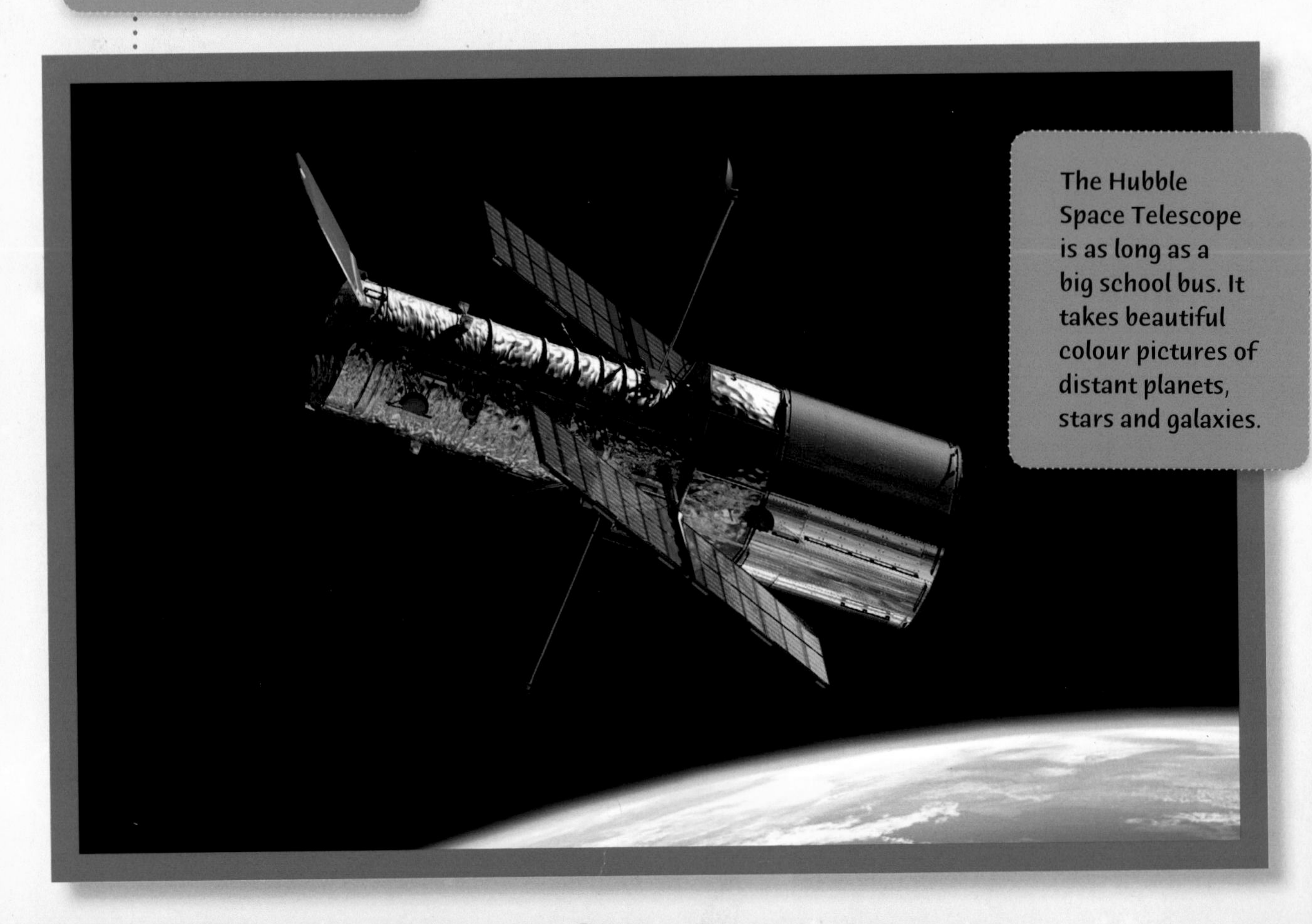

The Hubble Space Telescope is as long as a big school bus. It takes beautiful colour pictures of distant planets, stars and galaxies.

Spacecraft

Spacecraft that explore space include **probes**. These unmanned craft are launched into space and programmed to fly past planets or land on them. They send photos and other data back to Earth using radio signals. Some spacecraft carry people. In 1969 *Apollo 11* landed on the Moon and Neil Armstrong became the first person to walk on its surface. Moon missions have also brought rocks back to Earth! Today, astronauts go to places such as the International Space Station (ISS; right).

Buzz Aldrin (the second person to walk on the Moon) climbs down from the *Apollo 11* Lunar Module

Space stations

Space stations are giant structures that are put into space so that they orbit the Earth. Crews of astronauts and scientists live in them for weeks at a time. Space stations contain lots of equipment that is used to do experiments and to study objects in space. There are also other rooms where the crew sleep, eat and relax.

The ISS is a space station that orbits Earth.

Quick *FACTS*

- Space telescopes can see deep into space.
- The first person walked on the Moon in 1969.
- Lots of astronauts live and work on space stations.

? Which probe has travelled the furthest in space?
Turn the page to find out.

Inside *Voyager 1* there is a gold-plated record of greetings, images and sounds from Earth in case an intelligent life form finds it!

Exploring outer space

Voyager 1 is a probe that was launched in 1977 to visit Jupiter and Saturn. It took years to reach these planets. Since then it has flown past Uranus and Neptune. In 2013 it became the first spacecraft to leave our solar system. It still sends data back to Earth, but it is so far away it takes 17 years for its **radio signals** to reach us!

QUIZ TIME!

Voyager 1 has left the solar system and is now flying in the space between the stars. What is this space between the stars called?

a. outer space
b. interstellar space
c. intergalactic space

Answer on page 32.

Rocket power!

It takes a lot of energy for spacecraft to reach space. So they are attached to huge rockets, packed with rocket fuel, which blast them free of Earth's gravity. The Apollo spacecraft used rockets called Saturn V. When the rockets had finished firing, they would drop away and land in the sea so that they could be used again.

A Saturn V rocket blasts off to launch an Apollo spacecraft on a mission.

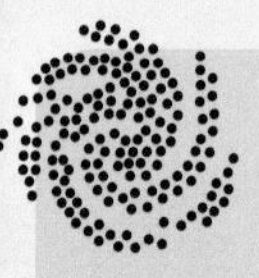

HAVE A GO **Find a radio with a long antenna and turn it to a quiet AM channel. Now jiggle a mobile phone near the antenna. The radio buzzes. The phone emits radio signals and the radio picks them up, rather like *Voyager 1*!**

Make this

Launch your own spacecraft using balloon power! The air being forced out of the balloon is stronger than the force of gravity, just like the rockets that launched the Apollo spacecraft.

Did you know that the Apollo spacecrafts were tiny? They would be the part near the tip of your model. The rest of the model is the rocket, called Saturn V.

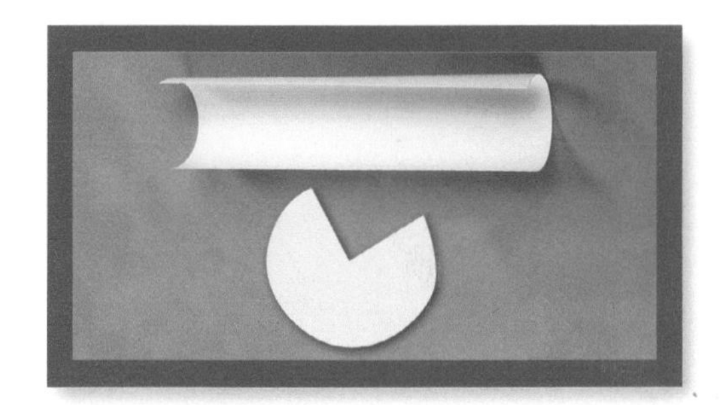

1 Roll a piece of card into a tube and tape it together. Cut a circle of card and cut a quarter section out of it. Roll the other three-quarter section into a cone that will fit the end of your tube. Tape it together.

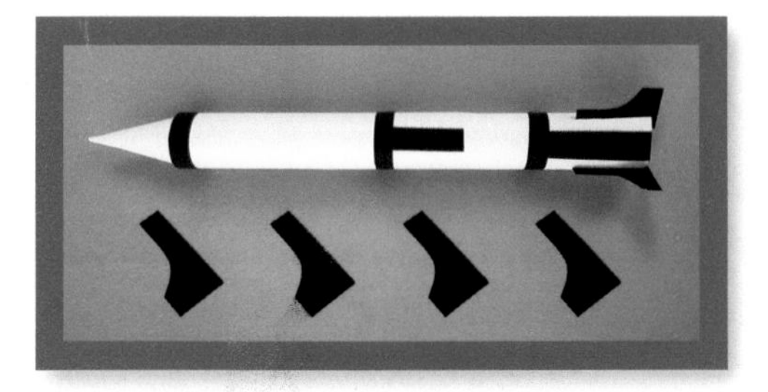

2 Attach the cone to one end of the tube. Cut out four black card fins as shown. Cut four slits in the bottom of the tube and slot in the fins. Decorate the tube with strips of black paper.

3 Thread a long piece of dental floss through a straight straw. (You'll need about 3 metres.) Tape the straw to the rocket.

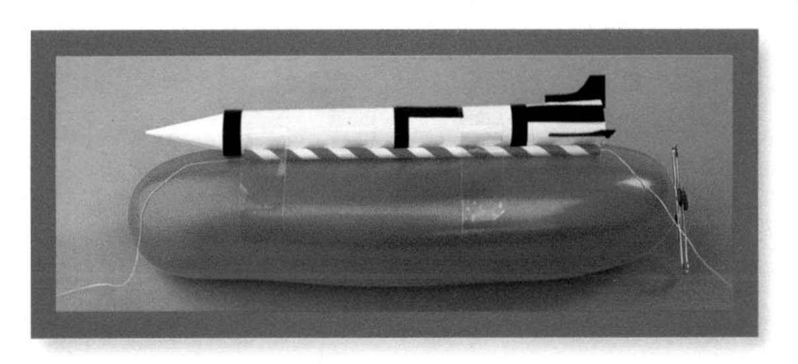

4 Blow up a long balloon and hold the neck closed with a paperclip. Tape the balloon securely to the straw.

5 To launch your rocket, attach one end of the dental floss to the top of a door (ask an adult to help you). Hold the other end of the floss near the ground – make sure the floss is tight. Take off the paperclip and watch your rocket fly!

GLOSSARY

astronomer scientist who studies the universe and the objects within it

atmosphere a layer of gases covering a planet

axis an imaginary line through the centre of an object

constellation a group of stars that look like a shape in the night sky when they are joined up

core the centre of something

dense thick or heavy for its size

energy power needed to make things work

evaporate the process that turns something from a liquid into a gas

force a push or a pull that makes things move in a particular way

galaxy huge group of stars, planets, dust, gas and other natural objects

gas substance, such as air, that is not solid or liquid

gravity force that pulls one object towards another

greenhouse gases gases, such as carbon dioxide, that trap heat in the Earth's atmosphere

hemisphere each half of the Earth, north and south of the Equator

liquid substance, such as water, that is not a solid or a gas

matter substance or material

myth a traditional story from a culture or people

orbit to travel around something

oxygen type of gas in the air that living things need to breathe

particle very tiny amount of matter

phases different stages that something goes through

probe in this instance, an unmanned spacecraft that transmits data about its surroundings

radio signal invisible signal that carries information through the air

solid something that is firm and holds its shape without help

spherical ball-shaped

telescope an instrument that uses lenses and mirrors to make things that are far away look closer

theory an idea about something

universe the whole of space and everything in it

BOOKS

Machines Close-up: Space Vehicles
by Daniel Gilpin (Wayland , 2012)

The Big Countdown: 70 Thousand, Million, Million, Million Stars in Space
by Paul Rockett (Franklin Watts, 2014)

***Fact Cat: Space* (series)**
by Alice Harman (Wayland, 2014)

Know It All: Space By Andrew Langley (Franklin Watts, 2014)

The Real Scientist: Space – Our Solar System and Beyond
by Peter Riley (Franklin Watts, 2012)

WEBSITES

http://www.nasa.gov/audience/forkids/kidsclub/flash/index.html
NASA's official site for kids.

www.kidsastronomy.com
Interactive pages, puzzles and games.

www.sciencekids.co.nz
Space-themed games, projects and videos of space shuttles blasting off!

http://wwwchildrensuniversitymanchester.ac.uk/interactivesscienceearthandbeyond
Another interactive site for space-mad kids.

http://www.bbc.co.uk/programmes/b019h4g8/features/calendar
Star charts from the BBC Stargazing Live site.

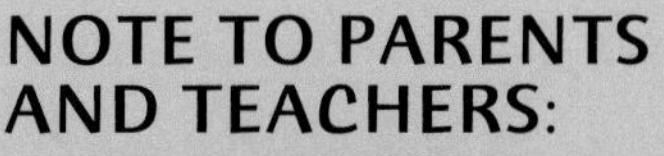

NOTE TO PARENTS AND TEACHERS:

Every effort has been made by the Publishers to ensure that these websites are suitable for children, that they are of the highest educational value, and that they contain no inappropriate or offensive material. However, because of the nature of the Internet, it is impossible to guarantee that the contents of these sites will not be altered. We strongly advise that Internet access is supervised by a responsible adult.

INDEX

QUIZ ANSWERS

Page 8. a – 8 minutes
Page 12. b – craters
Page 16. b – telescope
Page 20. a – global warming
Page 24. c – 400 times
Page 28. b – interstellar space